RECYCLED

To the CREATOR

Thank you for giving me a creative outlet.

RECYCLE: To recondition and adapt to a new use or function.

I WILL HOLD IT TIGHT

I will hold it tight, I will hold it close,

I will hold it long,

till it overflows.

I will not let it go;

I will not cease until it's complete.

It is real.

It is good.

It is alive.

It makes my soul speak and my heart beat.

My eyes carry it,

my lips sing it.

I will fight to keep it.

I will die before I forfeit it.

As breath enters and leaves my body and as my spirit lives,

forever will I hold it tight,

hold it close,

hold it long,

hold it in eternity.

Our love I will keep.

HEAR MY HEART

Hear my heart.

Hear it beat.

Listen closely.

Breathe silently.

Hear it speak.

You must have ears of love for you to hear,

better yet to comprehend that which lies within my heart.

Hear my heart:

It roars quietly,

Love me.

Can't you see the pure, innocent love that it bleeds?

If you look deep and listen closely, it will unleash all the treasures you've longed to see.

My heart won't hurt you.

Come in and see.

Let loose and be free in my heart.

YOU THINK I DON'T LOVE YOU

You think that I don't love you.

You're right—

I don't.

What you don't know is when you've gone off to sleep I get on my knees and thank God for you.

When you talk to me I get distracted because I'm busy visually tracing
you're lips so when we're apart I can always kiss you.

I run the ball of my fingers across your chest and back, and my prints
remember the touch of your skin so I'll always be with you.

When I look into your eyes, I see past your pupils into your soul
so I can become familiar with the truth about you.

Like when you act as if you are ok when your feelings are hurt or when you ask me
the question, *What am I going to do?* and I give you the answers I saw in you.

Right through you.

Into your soul, I saw your insecurities, strengths, and fears too.

You think sometimes I am cuddling you too much.

What I am really doing is listening to the orchestra of music your heart and spirit plays.

You don't know it, but I always show it.

You and only you have the ability to step into my presence and
make me drop everything I'm doing to tend to you.

That's why I get more accomplished when I'm not around you.

You are my autumn, my summer.

You are the physical beauty of my winter—the stillness and the pureness of the snow.

You have an unwavering power to always bounce back.

The stream of love you have for the life in others and your unselfish attitude,

You ignite a silent pounding wave of hope in me.

continued...

You think I don't love you—you're right, it's true.

I don't love you.

I life you. Passion you.

cosmic you.

Joy you.

Smile you.

Want you.

Free you.

Paranormal heart you.

Chest pounding, mind racing, body shaking you.

But I don't love you.

This generation's definition of love doesn't define what I have for you.

You and only you.

WE CAN DANCE

We can dance 100 dances to a thousand songs whispering a million *I love you*'s,

but that doesn't make it last.

At any moment I can become your past.

And all of the years we've cried together.

All of the heart break and mending.

All of the yelling and pain.

What we've worked up to,

the growth we've made it to,

can disappear and I can become a thing of your past.

Those years of silent prayers. Compromises and sacrifices for love
can be shoved back in the cave of your mind.

The passionate lovemaking ... the wide eyed adventures ... and success we've finally came to

can vanish, and like pencil to paper I can be erased,

and suddenly you're caressing a new face,

and I'm left standing with the echoes of a million *I love you*'s

and the *Trust me's I won't hurt you,*

the *Let me in's, I'm here for you,*

while you're with your new face, smiling, laughing, kissing, and making love,

doing the things I once thought made us special.

I can become a thing of your past at any moment.

So in this moment I'm going to hold on to you for dear life,

kiss you with every waking breath,

enjoy the softness of your skin, laugh at the wrinkle above your eye,

and breathe in the beauty of your life ...

because I never want to become your past.

TIMING

My heart is hurting.

It's skipping beats.

It bleeds out tears of pain, of loss and of grief.

Letting a love go that can no longer be.

A love that I want, a love that I WANT, a love that I can't have right now.

Everything is timing, and timing is everything, and our time is out of timing, so my heart bleeds tears.

I cry in my sleep.

I cry in my dreams.

I envision our life together, us with child.

Having a family you and I, and I begin to bleed, bleed out grief.

I am afraid if I don't take the opportunity to be with you, I'll never have you,

then I began to bleed; I bleed out loss.

When I look at your lips, I trace them in my mind.

I take a picture of your face with my eyes and hang it on the wall of my soul.

Your touch makes me feel safe.

Your voice helps me escape this world, and somewhere in-between heaven and earth we dance, but then I remember that timing is everything and everything is timing and our time is out of timing

and my heart begins to bleed.

Heavier than before, out pours tears, pain, loss, and grief.

Us. You and me. We.

Why didn't timing or destiny choose you ... and me?

Our timing, our destiny: it bleeds and bleeds ... it bleeds.

I SAID GOOD BYE

I said good-bye to you first in my spirit,

knowing that what we had would end soon.

I went along with it for a while, deceiving myself to believe it was going to work.

Through all of the trying and crying, yelling and anger, love and laughter, I stayed.

And when the seasons started to change, I quickly got ahold of my mind,

listening to you complain about what needed to change,

looking at the disappointment on you face each and every day put a sadness in my soul that I could

no longer face.

Falling asleep in one another's arms, we grew further and further apart.

We became like night and day.

When the communicating stopped and the *See you later* kisses came to a halt, I said good bye—

good-bye to you in my heart—

not losing love for you, just loving you in a completely different way,

crawling to your chest at night as you slept, laying down upon you softly
so as not to wake you, whispering my tearful good-bye.

To kiss your lips before we say it aloud.

To hug you one more time and grasp back the feeling that you were once mine.

My love, it is not your fault.

It's not mine either.

Some things must end so something else can begin.

We tried and it's not working, you and I.

However, you will always be my star and I your moon.

We will both shine loud.

We will both shine bright.

Just not together, but high in the vast space of the sky.

You were once mine and now I set you free, free to laugh, free to smile, free to grow, and free to be.

Good-bye, my love.

Good-bye, my star.

WHAT AM I TO DO

What am I to do when there is really no love behind *I love you*,

and when our talk time is nothing more than two sentences?

What am I to do when my heart breaks down every time you walk out the door?

What can I do because I can no longer deal with the fact that I've lost you?

The winds of time came to swoop you away, and there has been a
thundering storm outside the window of my heart ever since.

What am I to do?

What am I to do when I can't remember what it feels like to hug
or kiss you, but every night I lay beside you?

What am I to do when it hurts to breathe because with every sigh and release tears fall from me?

My love, what am I to do?

I am not used to life without you.

As the season changes, the look in your eyes does too.

There is no longer a look of joy or a sense of togetherness between you and I.

What am I to do?

Awake at night, pacing the floor, going over in my head what
could have been done or where did I go wrong.

Fumbling around in the reservoir of my soul is the question: My love, what am I to do?

Knowing the answer is that you are already gone.

There was a little birdie that came to whisper in my ear as I slept with tears rolling down my face.

He said, *Open the window of your heart and let fresh air in to clear the hurt away.*

Let the sun in your heart and come out to play.

This is your season to let it all go.

It is time for you, my dear, to grow.

My love, that is what you must do.

Never wallow in the past of what could have been done—move on and learn.

I LOOK FOR IT

I look for it in our kiss.

I look for it in our touch.

I look for it in the way we make love.

But love I never find.

For years we lie next to one another to sleep.

For years we laughed, cried, argued, and yelled.

For what?

For love's sake is what they say.

But love I never found in us.

Three years has passed—going on four—how long do we have to just be?

To coexist in a shared space with no real love, no real intimacy.

I know we care for one another's well-being; where is the love that makes you live in me and I in you?

I want what's real.

What's right.

What's mine.

What's for me.

I want the love that belongs to me.

BEATING MY HEAD

Beating my head against the covers,

my tears pounding against the pillow

as my hollow heart cries…

piercing sounds of the unspoken words *I love you*.

Being void of life. Life void of being. Being tangled in your intangible love.

You touch me and I melted in the past.

I touch you and you back away.

Where did I make the mistake?

It had to be me who messed up because you're too perfect.

See, I never had enough money for you.

Neither was my style fitting for your type.

I was never in the best shape for you, but my body never fell short of making you cum.

My lips never looked supple enough, but they held just the right
moisture to firmly place them around your penis.

I could never say we were together; the three years we lived together and the five
we spent together never qualified us as together. However, I coped.

You say I never gave you money. Maybe that's why I held no value to you.

I tried it, starting with hundreds and then a few thousand. It didn't change my value to you.

It just left me with another hole in my life—this time it wasn't my heart; it was my pocket.

I was never motivated enough, you say, therefore I couldn't motivate you…

I guess that's your excuse to do who you want to.

I didn't respect myself enough, you say; I guess that's why I don't get it from you.

You slept around while living in my home, then you told me if I
love you … I won't change; I would fight for you.

I fought for you, and lost more of myself.

I know I messed up … I do, because you're perfect and there's barely a flaw in you.

I miscarried myself by being involved with someone who had a premature outlook on love.

YOU CAN SMEAR THE MASCARA

You can look in the mirror and cry.

You can smear the mascara as you wipe your eyes.

You can tattoo that pain as a reminder of the lesson.

You've been weak and you let it show

You've been desperate and hurting—some things you won't let go.

You shared your feelings with the one who does not care and
gave your heart to the one who stripped it bare.

You've yelled out in excruciating pain.

You've held on in agony.

You've embodied the ridicule for your stupidity.

Your looks dwindled while you tried to keep up with hopeless love.

You walked around with your head up, but you were broken down.

Your words tried to maintain the fight, but inside you had already died.

Open to the pain and abuse, wounded in ways that you may no longer be of use.

In a financial deficit, not having a clue of what to do.

Your reflection in the window doesn't mirror you.

The image you worked hard to build has suddenly become something you just imagined.

Tired, bruised, and broken

... Heart utters words unspoken ...

Tragic happening.

Bad choices.

... Criticized by voices.

Taunting reality...

Dripping tears, yell for help.

A harsh reality, what a tragedy ...

I AM A VICTIM OF MY HEART

I am a victim of my heart

This bitch took off her bulletproof vest and let you shoot rounds at me.

Shots of lies and the constant misuse of the words *I love you*.

And those unforgettable moments of the times you cheated .

It wanted to hold on tight to loving you, when all I needed was this bitch to strap up,
shoot back and get the fuck out of Dodge from the bullshit you were shooting.

But oh no this bitch kept wanting more ... like a modern day whore.

Lies and cheating weren't enough.

She took in the times you compared her to other bitches like she
was common and anything but extraordinary.

But for some reason you gravitated toward the ordinary.

And this bitch didn't wave the white flag ...

she was holding on with double barrel shotgun holes in her ...

I mean, this bitch was leaking to death but somehow managed to fight for you with her dying breath.

Verbal , mental, and emotional abuse,

lies, cheating, and you acting as if this heart wasn't the shit and still that bitch held on to you.

She made me cry myself to sleep with pain only Jesus understood,

grieving about a relationship???!!

All the while I'm thinking, *What about us?*

What about our love,

wasn't it strong enough,

wasn't it deep enough?

Couldn't we, the two of us,

love us better than this man ever could ...

What about me?

How much further could we be if you had loved me that deep,

held on to me that long,

fought for me that strong,

loved me hard with your last dying beat.

continued...

How much better we could be.

I guess until you realize that I am worth the love,

you will keep accepting slugs in your heart ... from patty-cake marks who just want to leave scars ,men with no character, integrity, or understanding for what being a MAN truly is,

not understanding that you're a daughter of a queen.

Until you grasp that shit, you will always be one of these sorry-ass niggaz, bitch!

SLEEPING WITH YOUR BACK TURNED

You sleeping with your back toward me:

that used to bother me.

I have adjusted to the fact that we won't be.

[sings] *I can see clearly now the rain is gone.*

The rain of tears that lived in my eyes for years,

The pain in my soul,

the anger in my heart,

and the uncomfortable feeling of fear,

fear of losing you,

waking up one morning and you not being here.

That fear.

I have conquered that fear

and mastered the desire to be loved by no other then you.

It's true.

I wanted you to be the one I said *I do* to.

Yet lies and truth don't mix.

So I quit.

Quit wondering, worrying, hoping,

wishing, starting over,

talking and being open on purpose for this,

hard dick and bubble gum.

I can't even cum off of this.

I have come to the conclusion that you're losing because it's too much of *not enough love* in this mix.

I took this one to the chin.

Got this one with a broken nose,

swollen eye,

broken ribs.

To the soul, punches were what you were giving out.

continued...

When to find out the truth that the love we encountered I believed would last forever. However, I was wrong.

Dead wrong.

As dead as this relationship.

Yet alive as the grass grows as bright as the sunlight,

blooming like a flower and wonderful like a dream come true.

I found my way to a life without you.

A life in true love.

Not the sugared-up, watered-down love.

But I'm talking air-breathing, freedom-receiving, body-healing, soul-rejoicing, laugh-out-loud , fist-pounding, heart-racing kind of love

I found right inside of me,

right where I dropped it when I picked you up and put me down.

I found my greatest love in me.

So as you sleep with your back turned towards me, I have adjusted to the fact that we won't be, and tomorrow when you awake, I won't be here.

I won't be where you left me, put down.

Because I picked me up!

HIDING

Hiding behind your makeup, trying to cover up the scars on your heart.

The bruises and deep cuts that haven't healed but pus up.

Hiding behind the smile of *everything's just fine* to fight back a Nile river of tears.

I watched you paint your toenails that loud popping pink just to pace the floors.

All those nights of restless sleep and everything around you seeming so bleak.

You feel the pressure mount up against you, of your whole life and everything you've been through.

Stepping stones to success and demolition trucks that demolished your building blocks to success.

The stress.

Now you stand in the mirror with smeared mascara, fighting back the gripping pain of heartache.

No open door of escape.

Stumbling over questions,

looking for the door of answers, yet the road to your way out is too blurry.

So you hide behind your makeup to cover up the scars of your heart,

the bruises and deep cuts that haven't healed but pus up.

What do I do, where do I go from here?

So many lessons learned.

You realized you've been paralyzed by the toxic pain of heart wounds unhealed.

And you tried to cover it up by hiding behind your makeup.

But you wear it on your shirt and sleeves;

it spills over into your relationships and dreams;

now success is even farther away than it once seemed.

Every part of your being wants to scream,

yet you bleed silently behind your makeup,

with no exit of escape.

You've now become your own enemy.

tearing at your soul, frustrating your spirit and taunting yourself over what's done and what could've been.

continued...

Emotions boiling over.

You strip yourself of the makeup you hide behind.

You stand in front of a full body mirror and watch yourself bleed.

Looking at your wounds and deep cuts that pus up,

you wipe the tears that made the road to your way out too blurry.

Instead of makeup, you accept your wounds, mistakes, and the truth .

You are free to be healed. To be strong. To be wiser. No longer will you hide behind your makeup.

Makeup is now an expression of self love and joy instead of a cover-up.

WHO UNDERSTANDS BUT GOD

Who understands a woman's heart but you, God.

YOU.

I want to thank you, because you deconstructed my mind.

The way I saw things.

My heart you couldn't deconstruct because you weren't the one who constructed it.

My heart still wants what it wants.

You, the bruiser of hearts.

One that you didn't put in time to make.

You never held them right.

No hugs of love or kisses of passion, no pulse of pleasure to make it race.

You never caressed it the right way to make it feel safe ... secure.

It never rested in peace in your arms.

You abuser of hearts.

Yet you leave scars,

wounds so deep, you puncture places that can't be seen.

Did you hear that heart wakes up out of a cold sweat because of the devastating effect you left on it?

Did you happen to catch a glimpse of the tears that fell behind the smile?

Did you happen to see the stitches that you left behind when it saw your pain? It grasped you with compassion, and you broke it the first chance you got.

You breaker of hearts.

How dare you leave scars!

Tearing apart hearts you didn't create.

The creator pipes in glory. Installs forgiveness. Builds foundations of love.

He loves in purity so the heart could see past the in-between
and capture the visualization of your core being.

You abuser of hearts.

You heart breaker.

I would walk softly, speak low, and be honest.

The next heartbreak, God just may not let you get away with it.

continued...

You're tearing apart hearts so fast they can't be mended.

New hearts are on back order because what you left can't even be refurbished.

You're leaving girlfriends and moms to take out the trash you left behind.

I will say, *You are God's gift to the world.*

You forgot to equate in the equation that the HEART is GOD'S gift to himself.

You destroyer of God's gift,

how much pain and torment will you leave behind before you recognize that one true love,

that soulmate that everyone speaks of,

no longer exists for you?

You were like the Tasmanian Devil in destruction to demolish everything that bled for you.

In the process of your self-discovery on your quest to figure out shit,

While you clean and let go of your past so you could see clearer,

you blurred someone else's vision,

nearly killed someone else's dream.

One thing you did for sure, you tore my heart to pieces.

I couldn't recognize it—it was lifeless.

Good thing for you, my next one is like Apple's newest unreleased technology.

It beats harder. Sounds better. Loves wiser. Forgives quicker. More passionate than ever before.

To you, heart breaker,

Tread softly because Apple does, but hearts don't, have insurance packages.

God might just use you as insurance for his assurance this won't happen.

In lament terms the next one going to cost you.

I HAVE TRIED

I have tried. I have tried. I have tried.

Nothing seems to work out.

Over the past and the days yet to come,

I sit and stare, waiting for my change to come.

Tossing and turning at night.

No sleep and no peace.

I beat my inner self up, and now feeling worse than before, I yell out loud in the huge empty space of my home, CHANGE, WHEN WILL YOU COME?

Nothing I have done seems to work.

The empty, lost, longing feelings I have nearly bring me to tears.

The state of being alone, not knowing where you're going and longing for a future and a life that you dreamed of for many years.

Endured all of the hard times and all of its fears.

Lost battles but haven't lost the war, so I stand and demand for my change to come.

My life is at stake and my dreams are on the line.

When will you come, change?

What must I do or is there anything that can be done?

My sweat, my blood, my tears, and my years I have invested.

Yes, some things I have done foolishly, I admit,

but now time passes and my youth is far gone.

I can barely breathe in the coldness of the air as my pulse weakens and hands shake.

I sit, wait, and anticipate the coming of my change.

Change, when will you come?

WHO KNEW

Who knew pain could be so potent,

Or that you can cry carbon-black tears

Or smiles can shatter

Or that deception can sting like venom in your system

Or that infidelity can leave permanent scars.

Who knew that being hidden by someone you love could build an
indescribable issue that decided to take up residence in your soul.

Who knew that living in glass houses doesn't always mean you can see clearly

Or that love spelled backwards sounds like evil.

Who knew that the familiar doesn't always feel good.

Who knew that the longer you held on, the weaker you would become, and the
more you made your self available, the more distant he would get.

Who knew that closed captioned would mean reading what isn't clear with him.

Who knew that sometimes knowing the truth meant you would have to become a detective.

Who knew that standing on concrete floors with an verbally abusive
person, inevitably meant sinking in quick sand.

Who knew I would be pouring my heart and thoughts out to you with puffy eyes and snot-filled tissue.

Who knew that lobster and a broken heart goes good together.

Who knew that champagne could make disappointment taste so sweet.

Who knew that the beautiful woman that many men want and
women idolize would have been treated so poorly.

Who knew that falling down felt like death but the comeback set you high up with the Gods.

What I do know is that loving yourself first is not selfish.

Following your dreams means staying an individual.

Being beautiful starts within,

and CONFIDENCE says, YES I AM STILL THE SHIT, even after all of this!

STARTING OVER

Patches, stitches, sewn-together pieces. Stained fabric, bleached patterns, scuffed up sneakers. Blow Pops, ice cream trucks, rollerblades and beaches (starting over with new pieces).

Jean jackets, gold hoops, exotic fingernails. bustier picks, big hair, bright lips. Double Dutch, snapping fingers, loud tunes, middle finger screaming *I don't give a fuck* (fuck what u think about me).

Illest bitch, dope chick, Alaia latest shit. Silk blouse, Italian lingerie, champagne kisses, Brazilian waxed rose colored lips. Ambitious girl (I make my own rules).

Funky neon-red hair with a little bit of hot pink, big bowl of Cap'n Crunch, highlighters, markers, shades of color, paint brushes, and blank canvas. Short skirts, high-top leather Chucks, drumsticks, percussion sound, living life on a new beat, (I recycled the bullshit) this is the new me.

Starship, space status, scientific experiment, Mars movement, I'm the best type. Meteors, shooting stars, futuristic galaxy, galactic cannibalism, phenomenon, oxygen-filled dreams. Solar eclipse, midnight takeoff, off-radar trips. You don't know me (shame on you for having a distorted perception of me).

Vogue magazines, Paris-equipped runway pick, documentary life, whispers and chatters asking who's the new hit. Legendary looks, unforgettable style, printed life. Forbes 100 women you underestimated. Breaking story, this just in, accept it (I'M one of the illest women alive).

I AM

I can't be who I was.

I can't be who I've become.

Who I am I don't recognize or really like.

Who I was I've out grown.

There is no real place that I belong.

My wrapped arms around me doesn't feel like home.

A big world with circles inside smaller circles doesn't suit me.

I was never a circle girl or a click type.

I've always been a rider of the wind, a follower of the stars, and a friend of God.

That inside core part of me has napped long enough.

A roaring of change with hurricane lessons learned has turned me into HER.

Separating the destruction from what could be salvaged has shown me
that the God in me is bigger than their stares and chatter.

Her urge to be the wings that held up the sky is what separated her from those who wanted to fly.

And those space walkers— she differentiates herself by knowing that space is what she needed

and heaven is where she resides, but being is where she belongs because her existence is her own.

Too many have tried to define her.

Box her in.

But she passed the blessed test.

So as they become more aquatinted, I, her and me.

Monumental overload is where those circles within circles and clicks
wreck their level-headed brains to understand her.

She was never level-headed because levels can't exist when you live in dimensions.

There is strength in numbers.

As I, her, and me, we become one.

We will be brighter than the sun, yet still the substance of the universe, like water to the earth

I Am that I AM!

CONTACTS

Looking through my contacts because I couldn't contact you.

Trying to find a name that would replace you.

But your voice was too deep.

That baritone–tone penetrated to my bones, so I couldn't break away from you.

Coming in contact with faces to fill the spaces when you left and took my belongings that you had no rights to; I or my heart or things of that matter didn't matter to you.

I couldn't contact you.

I was always available 24-7, 365 days, make that 366 during leap year.

I didn't know I was just another contact because the way we made contact when we made love was something extraterrestrial to me,

and we both agreed that what we had was more than just physical but mental and spiritual.

I thought our love could go to INFINITY and BEYOND and the knowledge we acknowledged about one another was light years compared to our past experiences with other lovers.

The limited contact that we were making had me unstable.

I suffered withdrawal, had a dose of paranoid delusion because in my mind there was another.

I couldn't bear it:

comparing the way we connected when we made contact, that you may do the same with another lover.

See, my connection was cosmic and your galactic love was powerful.

We shared insights about life. We bonded over hard times. We cried during the molding of change.

And sparked when we both started following our dreams.

So why did it seem that our contact was out of context?

You carried around with you different means of contact, but I only had one way of connecting with you.

I discovered there were far too many personal contacts you kept.

You assured me that there was no other.

So why were we constantly losing our connection. Breaking up. Our signal fading in an out till our lines got crossed and others intercepted our connection.

continued...

Soon I was wasn't able to contact you at all.

You became mythological, and I started to think I imagined you.

But the electromagnetic force between you and I left an electric charge in my body, and I couldn't deny your existence. I went out of my way to get us reconnected, and this time we would make sure that when we made contact we would never become disconnected.

MOVING FORWARD

Subject: Fwd:

What you want from your mate is inspiration.

I stopped being the epitome of your light when I stopped living
in expectation of what I wanted for my life.

Instead I turned my fuel to you and looked to you to be the spark that ignited my flame.

When you weren't, it literally drove me insane.

Like a dish on a menu they chose to discontinue, you and I discontinued our love for one another.

Now love has become something we fight ourselves to give to one other.

Bitter quarrels. Bruised and damaged hearts.

Disappointed remarks.

Silent tears and upside-down smiles are what linger now.

But I'm not finished yet!

See, you pulled back layers of my ego and made me love you more than any man I've ever known.

You pushed me to my limit of love, which made me in turn find that true love has no limits.

You tested my ability to forgive and forget,

to let go of bitterness and resentment.

You made me so vulnerable I got scared.

You made me realize that true love takes compromise and sacrifice,
not of one's beliefs, but of the one you believe in.

I know that I don't run on empty, and I am not nor should I ever be the epitome of your light,
But another peak to have a different view of the light that already shines through you.

We are not one another's source, but we've been blessed to be acknowledged
as an option of resource for one another's life projects.

With this new beginning, rather, you chose to accept it with me or not.

I will be the fuel, and my desire to leave my mark shall be my flame.

You will be your own inspiration because you will be busy inspiring others.

Rather, we take the turn to friends instead of lovers.

I know that you will never find another, but you will always be happy because
my love, which is Great, which is Deep, Honest and Pure, will always be
with you to push you to make power moves, to always do you.

continued...

Let's stop breaking hearts and destroying emotions.

Let's build together worlds that leave OUR legacy, that Truth and the drive
to be better are what changed us from enemies to friends.

From friends to companions.

Companions to lovers.

From lovers to the essence of what true love should be.

You and I living life beyond each other's limitations boundless in bliss.

You and I survived our own self-patronizing enemies and learned to live out our dreams.

SORRY

I said sorry to everyone I feel I've hurt except you.

I was so focused on the person I loved, I forgot to love you.

I stood by and watched them say rude things to you and be mean; I saw how it affected you.

I listened to you beat yourself up, watched you get depressed, and listened to
you tell me of the many thoughts of suicide that ran across your mind. I always
knew you wouldn't do it. But I never gave you encouragement.

When he came into your life I watched you fade away. I should
have come by and maybe I would not have lost you.

When you were no longer working and put your dreams on hold,
I knew that it killed you. I should have fed you life.

The worst was when that guy—the one you loved and trusted—cheated on you; I knew you didn't
have a lot of strength left to pick yourself up and leave. My job was to come rescue you. I didn't.

I saw you cry repeatedly; even when you smiled, the tears rolled
down your face. I was supposed to be your strength.

I didn't hold your hand when you were scared or tell you, *You are beautiful*. I didn't tell you, *I love you*.

You made me laugh.

You made me want to live life to the fullest.

The excitement in your voice for your dreams made me believe.

I wasn't there for you.

I didn't take care of you.

I put others before for you

I let you and watched you die.

I wasn't the voice of reason for you.

I should have made you take responsibility for what you accepted, and I know I wouldn't have lost you.

I should have told you it wasn't all of his fault and that you are responsible for
what you allow and how you are treated. That you are no one's victim.

I know for sure you would have made the necessary changes you needed to, to better you.

continued...

BUT I promise you, as you resurrect yourself,

I will be with you.

I will never leave you.

I will always trust you.

We will be strength together.

We will never fade away.

No man will ever come between us.

You and I are here to stay.

I love you and will never stop telling you.

You are my most precious and valued friend.

You are beautiful and I miss you.

I said sorry to everyone I feel I've ever hurt.

But I've never said sorry to you (myself). I am sorry.

I love you

FRIEND

I have never had a friend like you.

I love you.

I never want to be without you.

My heart will bleed if you leave.

Night and day I scream your name.

In the morning, I awake with puffy eyes to see you still by my side.

You fight with me.

You comfort me.

You tell me the truth and when I do the opposite of your good counsel, you never call me a fool. Instead you say, *I love you.*

How could I ever be without you?

My being is knitted to your spirit—can you feel it?

My heart beats.

Quietly, my soul speaks.

My rising sun.

My blooming flower.

I love you honestly, openly, and freely.

I love you, Lord.

Thank you.

TO THINE OWN SELF BE TRUE

To thine own self be true.

It wasn't out of the blue the things you allowed yourself to go through.

I can't quite pinpoint where it all started.

Somewhere along the way you lost your voice.

You relinquished your power and didn't follow your inner desire.

There is no one to blame but you.

To thine own self be true.

Oh my how you allowed yourself to be abused in more ways than one,

and in more ways than one your life shifted and changed, and there never was a good outcome.

Sure there were blessings along the way, yet looking back over all of this shit, was it worth it?

The fucked-up relationships and the time wasted on sticking it out, trying to make them work.

Losing yourself in the midst.

I have to wonder, *What are you really afraid of?*

You haven't launched out into the deep and followed your dreams.

You made small attempts that would separate a cat from a kitten or a cub from a bear,

but not from those who really want it and those who go out and take it.

To thine own self be true.

I never apologized to you.

I never really forgave you.

I never really showed you what it is and feels like to love you.

To love us.

Why haven't you ever trusted what we're made of?

I question whether am I too far gone from my true essence to grip myself into a new reality.

I love the tougher you.

But it's really the hurt you who's just not going to take it anymore.

Back then we discussed men. We discussed how this one came in and destroyed you.

We chuckle now because we've grown enough to know we were not victims.

continued...

Victims don't have a choice

You always had one with him.

Thank you so much for accepting responsibility in the part you
played in allowing yourself to be mistreated.

To thine own self be true.

You are beautiful.

I'm not talking about that kind of beauty that captures attention.

But the kind that changes the soul.

You are intelligent, not the kind that spent years in college.

But the kind that voluntarily reads Walt Whitman, Thomas Pynchon, Jean Genet, and Ayn Rand.

The kind that grasps a deeper understanding of the world and the people in it

Your sensitivity eludes this world into the spirit, and you not only feel it but submit to it.

You are tangible, but the great things about you can't be touched or reached but felt deep.

I owe this to you. It's loooong overdue. My love, my dear, I apologize to you for all I've done and
neglected to do. My breath of peace and strength of hope, I forgive you for what you put us through.

From me to myself, this is my letter to you: To thine own self be true.

To thine own self be true.

TO THINE OWN SELF BE FOREVER TRUE.

PEACE

Kitchen cabinets, refrigerator doors, oven knobs, and hallway floors!

Light bulb fixtures, air conditioners.

White-painted walls over red-painted hearts.

Loud speakers, bass sounds over screaming words saying, *This is the last time*.

Brooms and dust pans sweeping up shattered dreams.

Mops and buckets washing over jar-filled spilled tears

Medicine cabinets, soft facial tissue, index-finger-written words on
steamed mirrors saying, *2nd chances come with learned lessons*.

Symphony self-written memories of the ideal me, basking in the glory of the journey.

Faucet-filled water filters, closet hangers, and curtains,

Boxed-up ideas that need to be reopened.

Old empty house with aerobic DVD of the shed dead weight of all the BS that stuck itself to me.

New address. Shipments of new smiles. Echoes of laughter. New space. Fresh, soft linen.
Fluffed, firm pillows. Bright, calm-colored room. Finally peace has found me.

BROKEN AT IT'S BEST

Broken diamonds on shattered glass floors, with mangled hearts hanging from the ceiling.

Wonder in the eyes of the lives unlived.

Beauty emerges from the oddest places, and a new point of view comes from
those dark places where tears had a way of washing those dim layers.

Cracked glass now seems to be a gleaming sparkle of rainbows.

And broken diamonds now show you that nothing last forever.

Accepting that inner peace,

reevaluating your self value,

rebuilding trust within yourself,

and realizing that liquid gold is found in the jars of your hard times.

New memories are made when you let go of the past.

Bright futures are found stuck between the cracks of those old
wooden attic floors where no one ever looked.

It's kinda funny that when you find new love it's been there this
entire time, right between your own two arms.

Gems are what they call people like you, and gazing is what they do with that gleam they see in you.

It's a chuckle you get in the pit of your belly when life took you on one
of the scariest journeys and gives you an unimagined end.

Then God shows up and shakes his head at you for having so little trust.

Those broken diamonds on shattered glass floors and mangled hearts
hanging from ceiling fans now look like van Gogh paintings.

You can see the pain, yet there is a beauty that only the soul and spirit can understand.

It's a picture of the past but the present keeps moving.

BEAUTIFUL

Beautiful heartbeats and pale faces.

Loud colorful laughter. Unordinary features. Magnetic love. Lightning-bolt energy.

You have that wonderful way about you.

You have an orgasmic type of feel to you.

You are so sensitive you feel everything to the point you're connected to all things.

The way you read me gets me weak.

You see how I most times doubt myself; we laugh because we both know
that I am remarkably strong and independently creative.

You have this powerful, heavenly kind of belief where you believe anything is possible.

You have this reach past the stars into uncharted territory kind of faith.

there is this unbelievable healing that takes place in silence.

I will never forget that you taught that to me.

Your Einstein quotes on human life and Aristotle's poetic philosophy always somehow
make me think life really isn't a mystery ... it's an open book of self-discovery.

You open my eyes and remind me to live.

You knew I was hurt bad, and seen I was fragile, you somehow managed
to see that tiny, flawed weak spot and gave it a sparkle.

I didn't know pale faces and beautiful heartbeats could create priceless paintings.

When you loved life into me, it was like taking the most wonderful things from around
the world and throwing them on a nude canvas to make an abstract piece of art.

Loud, colorful laughter and unordinary features, beautiful heartbeats, and pale faces.

A kinetic spirit gave me a new life worth living!

FINALLY

Finally I can laugh loudly.

Live freely.

Completely and totally be me.

My smile is bigger.

My inner light is brighter.

The air seems so much fresher and nothing is unattainable.

I am free, emotionally free, from the past.

I am free to live in the present and plan for the future.

I am happy, I am at peace, the inner struggle, the inner war, the victory I spent years fighting for, I have now won!

Hurray!

I am free.

Free to dance my dance. To sing my own tune. To live out loud.

My being rejoices in this freedom.

My soul swims in praise, my eyes cry tears of appreciation.

My lips open loudly and my voice roars.

I am as free as a cloud, as bright as the sun.

My beauty is as vast as the sky

My uniqueness is as the many colors and flowers.

Like the marine life in the ocean and across the sea, like the century old and current, I am undiscovered beauty.

In this world I am finally free.

Thank God Almighty

I am free!

Free at last, thank God Almighty

I am free at last

LOVE

Last night, I fell in love.

I fell into being free.

I fell into me.

I chased after change,

ran from hell,

fought for life,

and bumped into healing.

And for the first time in history I felt love's soft hands brush across my skin.

I saw it smile from the inside out.

I sat next to it,

reached in front of it to taste the sweetness of its kiss.

Last night, love played a melody for me with its heartbeat as we danced slowly upon rose petals.

Last night as I gazed upon the bright stars,

I saw an illuminating glow that came from within me.

It was love cleansing and healing me.

I went to sleep in a blissful peace.

When I awoke, love wasn't lying next to me.

This morning when I awoke I found love.

Living,

breathing,

beating,

right inside of me.

Last night, I fell totally, completely, and irrevocably in love with me.

NEW BEGINNING

It is passion that ignites the fire of hope
and complex pieces that drives us to find the answers of the commonly-asked question, *Why are we here?*
It is fantasy that keeps us out of touch with reality.
It is unrealized dreams that keep us chasing change.
It is self-growth that changes those around us.
It is the quieting of our souls that we hear the most truth.
It is stepping into the new where we find we have talents we never knew.
It is the starting over that disappoints us, but it is embracing it that propels us.
It's the journey that excites us.
It is the moments that join us and the memories that keep us.
It is in broken hearts that we find self healing.
It is in the times we feel most lost that we redefine ourselves.
It is the power of knowing who we are that sustains us.
It is the light that we hide selfishly inside that keeps us from the true glory of life.
The sun rises to shed light on all that is hidden.
The moon rises to declare that only those who truly want it will find it in the dark.
It is the Latin words NOVUS INITIUM spoken into my spirit where
I truly allowed myself to embrace a new beginning.

Recycling turns materials that would otherwise become waste into valuable resources

re·duced, re·duc·ing, re·duc·es

1: To bring down, as in extent, amount, or degree; diminish.

2: To bring to a humbler, weaker, difficult forced state or condition;

re·use re·used, re·us·ing, re·us·es

1: To use again, especially after salvaging or special treatment or processing.

Sometimes a fourth R is added to the three basic ones, generally standing for either **"rethink" or "recover."**

"Rethink is sometimes added to the front of the hierarchy, meaning that we should consider our options and think about their impact

re·think thinks, -thinking, -thought re·thought (-thôtre·think·ing,

1: To think about (something) again, esp with a view to changing one's tactics or opinions.

2: To reconsider (something) or to involve oneself in reconsideration.

Recover, which is the last R, refers to

re·cov·er·y

1: an act of recovering the regaining of or possibility of regaining something lost or taken away.
Restoration or return to any former and better state or condition. To get back; regain.

2: To restore (oneself) to a normal state

Recycled

www.ingramcontent.com/pod-product-compliance
Lightning Source LLC
Chambersburg PA
CBHW040258100426

42811CB00011B/1305